M000188910

What I Wish I Knew
When I Was in ...
High School

55 Secrets **EVERY** Student Needs to Know about Succeeding in School, Leadership, and Life

By Jerry Franklin Poe

About Jerry Franklin Poe

 **Jerry Franklin Poe** is the founder of Poetential Unlimited LLC, a company designed to train and equip the mind, activate the vision, cultivate the passion, and hone the skills necessary to live life on your terms.

Jerry turned his passion for personal growth and development into a life mission of showing individuals and organizations how to achieve their purpose and goals in life.

As a well known speaker, Jerry has delivered over 2,900 empowering presentations to schools, colleges, and organizations across North America. Jerry has spent the last 14 years working in higher education, leadership consulting, and motivational speaking. Jerry uses real-life experiences, stories, and analogies to educate, equip, inspire, and entertain his audience.

Jerry has authored two books and is a certified life and business coach.

www.JerryPoe.com

Schedule Jerry Franklin Poe to Speak at Your Event

(484) 301-0763

www.JerryPoe.com

Your Ideal Speaker for:

- Conference Keynotes
- Conference Workshops
- Black History Month
- Greek/Panhellenic Events
- Leadership Retreats
- Orientations
- Student Government Programs
- Summer Programs

Top 3 Most Requested Topics:

1. *What I Wish I Knew about Being a Great Student Leader*
   - How to become a better leader and difference maker on your campus
2. *What I Wish I Knew about Excelling in School*
   - Ideas that will put you ahead of your class from Day One
3. *What I Wish I Knew about Building a Profitable Career*
   - How to become the employee companies love to hire

Special Bonus

Schedule Jerry and receive 100 FREE BOOKS

Empower and Equip Others!
Share this Book

What I Wish I Knew When I Was in ... High School

55 Secrets EVERY Student Needs to Know about Succeeding in School, Leadership, and Life

How great would it be if you were given a manual to guide you through every aspect of your life that lay ahead of you? Give yourself the winning edge. Crack the code to success in school, leadership, and life by reading the tips shared throughout this book. These quick tips are easy to read, understand, and more importantly apply immediately. Go ahead and get started!

Special Quantity Discounts

2 – 20 Books	$15.00 ea.
21 – 99 Books	$14.00 ea.
100 – 499 Books	$13.00 ea.
500 – 999 Books	$12.00 ea.
1000+ Books	$11.00 ea.

To Place an Order
Call (484) 301-0763

www.JerryPoe.com

Everyone is Reading Jerry's Books

Stedman Graham

Educator, Author, Businessman, & Speaker

Joe Theismann

Super Bowl Champ, Redskins QB, & NFL Analyst

Glenn Morshower

TV & Movie Actor: *24*, *Transformers*, & *X-Men*

www.JerryPoe.com

Why I Wrote the Book Series

"I wish I knew" is a phrase we hear all the time. I know I have said it countless times over the years. I bet you have said it as well. If we had a time machine, we could travel back and enlighten our younger selves. The reality is no one can go back in time. However, I decided to do the next best thing ... share the wisdom of my life experience with the next generation.

My objective is to assist as many young people as possible and help them become well rounded, productive citizens. If I had understood these life lessons, strategies, and suggestions in my youth, I could have saved myself a lot of heartaches and headaches.

I hope you appreciate the information shared throughout this book and apply it to your life.

- Jerry Franklin Poe

"Faith is the key to unlock
the results you desire."

- Jerry Franklin Poe

Secret #1

Beat the Bell

Every aspect of our lives is run by a clock. Being on time is good. Being early is even better. Develop the habit of beating the school bell. Arrive at school before the bell rings. Arrive at your next class before the bell rings. This habit of being early rather than on time or late will serve you for the rest of your life.

How you manage your life in relationship to time will determine the impressions people have of you. In our society, we think about people who are late a certain way. We identify certain character traits with those who show up late. What impression do you want to create? How do you want people to see you?

When you plan to be early rather than on time, you also are better prepared for any unexpected challenges that might occur. Murphy's Law usually kicks in when you least expect and least want it to.

In your schedule, plan to always arrive early.

"Nothing splendid has ever been achieved except by those who dared believe that something inside of them was superior to circumstance."

- Bruce Barton

Secret #2

We're All Leaders

It does not matter who you are.

It does not matter what organization you are a part of.

It does not matter where you fall in the hierarchy.

Recognize you are a leader. Right now. Today.

There is someone looking to you for guidance—which makes you a leader.

There is someone looking at you as an example to follow—which makes you a leader.

You are leading every day of your life. You do not need to wait for someone to appoint you to a position. Know you are a leader and act like one.

You are a leader in your life. You are a leader in your family. You are a leader within your community.

You were born to lead.

"*Now if you are going to win any battle you have to do one thing. You have to make the mind run the body. Never let the body tell the mind what to do.*"

- General George S. Patton

Secret #3

The Power of Gratitude

Take a moment and think about where you were in life a year ago. I bet you are much farther along in your journey than you even realize or give yourself credit for.

Give yourself credit for all you have accomplished thus far. Gratitude is an important part of attraction. Think about it. When you give someone a present, their level of gratitude and thanksgiving will determine how much you give them next time. If a person is really appreciative of what you have done for them, it makes you want to give them more and more. However, if they were to say, "Is this all I get? Didn't you see all the items on my wish list?" would you want to give them more?

Take stock of your accomplishments, appreciate yourself, and be thankful for where you are now.

"Men are anxious to improve their circumstances, but are unwilling to improve themselves; they therefore remain bound."

- James Allen

Secret #4

Recognize Your Strengths & Your Weaknesses

Identifying your strengths and weaknesses is extremely important in becoming successful.

If you work on developing your strengths, then you can operate in excellence.

If you work on developing your weaknesses, then you can improve them and most likely become good at them.

We recognize people for excellence not for being good at something. There are many people who are good ... very few who are excellent.

Therefore focus on strength development and strategic partnerships for your weaknesses. When working on a group or team project, look for classmates who complement you rather than compete with you. A competitor is someone who is strong in the same area as you. Someone who is strong in an area where you are weak is a complement to you. For example, if you are weak in the area of public speaking, organization, research, etc., then find classmates who are strong in the areas to complement your strengths.

> *"The mold of a man's fortune is in his own hands."*
>
> *- Francis Bacon*

Secret #5

Stand Up for What Is Right

Great leaders take a stand. They stand up for what they believe in. They stand up for what is right.

Great leaders do not allow fear of negative attacks or opposition to deter them from doing the right thing.

If you allow fear to prevent you from standing up for what you know to be right, then you are lowering your standards to please others. Once you turn your back on your own beliefs and values, it becomes easier to continuing doing so in the future.

Take a stand. Let your voice be heard.

"Circumstances do not make the man, they reveal him."

- James Allen

"The difference between a successful person and others is not a lack of strength, not a lack of knowledge, but rather in a lack of will."

- Vincent T. Lombardi

Secret #6

Positive Self-Talk Makes a Difference

Monitor your self-talk.

We all talk to ourselves. If you do not believe you talk to yourself, you are probably asking yourself right now, "Do I talk to myself?" and the answer would be yes, you do. The question is, what do we say to ourselves and what do we think to ourselves?

Not all of our self-talk is positive, and the reason why is that we have been programmed to talk negatively to ourselves. How we talk to ourselves is based on how people talked to us. How you learned to speak as a child was based on how your parents spoke. You modeled what you saw.

When you were a child, people said things to you that weren't always positive, and eventually these things started to become your own talk. When it was time for you to want to do something, you said to yourself, "Oh, I can't do it." Why? At some point in the past somebody told you that you couldn't do it.

Write down all the things you say to yourself. Examine your statements to find the cause or the root for why you are saying them. This process will provide you a track record of what you have been saying or thinking.

"The words you speak shape the world you live in." – JFP

"If you keep on saying things are going to be bad, you have a good chance of becoming a prophet."

- Isaac Bashevis Singer

Secret #7

Attend Summer School

Go to summer programs designed for high school students to gain college experience.

- Upward Bound
- Upward Bound Math Science

Also, go to summer programs designed for incoming college freshmen. This will enable you to become comfortable with the campus. It will also build up your GPA because you will get to take a few classes before the fall semester gets started.

"*When dealing with people, remember you are not dealing with creatures of logic, but with creatures of emotion.*"

- Dale Carnegie

Secret #8

Look for the Best in Others

Challenge yourself to find something you like about everyone you meet.

This will compel you to start thinking differently because most of our interpretations or perceptions of people have been based off of our past programming. When you see people, you automatically form a thought about them. What you are going to do now is check your programming.

So as soon as you get your very first impression, you challenge it by asking yourself, "Is this impression of them true or not true?" If you do not like what you are thinking, then ask yourself, "What else could I think about them?"

Use your creative power, your imagination, to come up with things that are positive, which will change your perception of them.

So instead of saying, "I do not like that person," try to think of things that you could like. Ask yourself, "What could I like about them?"

This does not mean you have to spend a lot of time with them. All you are doing is changing how you think by saying, "I want to find the good in people rather than the bad."

> *"I will speak ill of no man, and speak all the good I know of everybody."*
>
> *- Benjamin Franklin*

Secret #9

It Is Okay to Fail

If you haven't failed at something, then you are spending too much time in your comfort zone.

Life uses failure to teach us. It is how we learned to walk. You had to fall a few times first, before you could make it across the floor.

Fail and Learn. This is the sequence to remember.

Failure is a learning opportunity. Failure is a chance to move forward in life.

When you fail, learn from what happened. Move on to the next thing.

"Failure is only the opportunity to more intelligently begin again."

- Henry Ford

Secret #10

Join the Right Clubs

There are many clubs at your school. All of them are great; however, all are not right for you.

When you are picking which clubs to join, think about how the club will influence and inspire you to grow and mature as a person, as a leader, and as a student.

You want to think about what you will bring to the group. But the more important factors are ...

- Who you will become as an active member of the club?
- How will the club help you improve?
- What you will learn from the club?

Secret #11

Prepare for the Next Level in Life

Always think about the next level in your life journey. Regardless of what direction your journey is taking you (college, career, military), look for ways to develop habits and skills that will enable you to succeed at the next stage in your progression. You want to develop a long-term vision for your life. Build success, leadership, and life skills that transfer and apply to the opportunities you will encounter in the future.

Always schedule time in your day to think about what is next for you and ask yourself, "What do I need to learn, understand, and develop to succeed on that level?"

"Destiny is not a matter of chance, it is a matter of choice."

- Oliver Wendell Holmes

Secret #12

Talent Is a Gift, Skill Is Developed

Talent is what you are born with.

Skill is something you develop in life.

Talent can only take you so far. At some point you need to turn your talent into skill.

Skill is the ability to successfully perform a task under pressure and with opposition.

In order to maximize your talent and develop skills, you will need to be disciplined. Practice is important. Practice makes permanent. Shape your talent into useful skill sets you can use to build the lifestyle you desire.

"Talent is not entitlement. It's how you use, sharpen, and express your talent that will determine the results you produce in life." - JFP

Secret #13

Get Organized & Develop Systems

Being organized as a student will help you stay on top of your tasks, projects, and schedule.

You want to find or develop a system for organizing your life as a student. Also find or develop a system for note-taking and studying.

Being organized and systematic is critical to developing good study habits.

> *"To do two things at once is to do neither."*
>
> *- Publilius Syrus*

Secret #14

Learn to Relate to People

The art of building rapport is a very important quality of a leader. Everyone has a different point of view, personality, and communication style. Look for the common ground.

What part of your personality matches up with theirs?

What viewpoints do you share?

You want to create a "me too" experience for the people you interact with. They should be able to see themselves in you.

Accentuate the commonalities you have with people. Listen for what is important to them. Concentrate on your similarities.

"Everyone likes a compliment."

- Abraham Lincoln

www.JerryPoe.com

Secret #15

You Are Perfect in Your Imperfection

Get rid of the illusion of normalcy.

Get rid of the illusion of perfection.

Recognize everyone is unique. Therefore you are only normal to yourself—which means everyone is abnormal to everyone else.

You are perfect the way you are. Your imperfection is your perfection.

Be yourself. You are the only one who can. The world needs you to show up. The world does not need a copy of somebody else.

"Know and believe in yourself, and what others think won't disturb you."

- William Feather

Secret #16

Be Well Rounded

Being able to relate to people has a lot to do with what you have experienced and explored in life. Don't get stuck in one area of the school experience. Mix things up.

Find a sport you can participate in. Look for ways to express yourself in the arts and music department. Learn about different cultures, societies, and religions.

The more you learn and experience things outside your comfort zone, the more well rounded and cultured you become. You then develop an appreciation for the diversity this world has in music, art, culture, people, etc.

"Man's mind once stretched by a new idea, never regains its original dimension."

- Oliver Wendell Holmes

Secret #17

Quickly Adapt and Be Flexible

How well do you deal with change? Coping with change is a natural part of leadership. Those who adapt the fastest and remain flexible succeed the most.

Change cannot be avoided. It is something you need to anticipate and be prepared for.

Learn to make adjustments in the moment. Do not be attached to one way of doing things.

"It is not the strongest of the species that survive, nor the most intelligent, but the one most responsive to change."

- Charles Darwin

Secret #18

The Internet Doesn't Have an Eraser

Technology develops faster than the social world it serves. There are so many ways to communicate and interact online. The ability to instantly communicate and socialize with countless numbers of people worldwide is great; however, one click can cause lots of damage that can last for a lifetime.

Once you hit "send," "update," etc., you cannot get it back. You have no idea who will see it, forward it, or share it with others. Content on the Internet has a way of coming back to haunt you. So be careful about what you put out there.

Think about how you want to be seen or perceived long term. Something you post online today can impact your future opportunities in higher education and in your future career.

Remember, the Internet has no eraser.

Secret #19

Make Homework a Top Priority

The first thing you need to tackle when you get home from school should be your homework. Once you have finished, then you can focus on all the other activities you love to engage in.

One of the biggest mistakes I made in high school was procrastinating on my homework and school projects. When you make homework the top priority, you give yourself the best chance of completing your assignment with less pressure and stress. You will not be rushed to get things done during homeroom the next morning in school.

By making homework a top priority you give yourself enough time to focus on challenging task and projects—which will give you an opportunity to ask for help when you need it and a better chance at a higher grade.

> **"No one can make you feel inferior without your consent."**
>
> **- Eleanor Roosevelt**

Secret #20

Beware of the Clique

Being a part of a select group can be a positive and negative experience.

Check yourself ...

- What does the group have you doing?
- How does the group affect who you are as a person?
- Do you like the person you are becoming?
- Do they accept you for who you really are? Or are you changing who you are to fit in?
- Is it worth it?

Be aware of the trap of trying to fit into a group.

You were made an original for a reason. Find people who will appreciate your uniqueness and individuality.

"Self-image sets the boundaries of individual accomplishment."

- Maxwell Maltz

> **"The only limit to our realization of tomorrow will be our doubts of today."**
>
> **- Franklin D. Roosevelt**

Secret #21

Build a Dream Wall

At some point in your life, you have probably heard the phrase, "Seeing is believing." One way to believe you can achieve the results you desire is to build a dream wall.

Create a visual image of the lifestyle you desire to experience in the future.

1. Get a big piece of paper or poster board.
2. Put/Paste a picture of yourself in the middle.
3. Cut out pictures of things that represent the future lifestyle you desire to experience (places you want to travel to, college you want to attend, career you want to have, etc.).
4. Paste the pictures around the picture of yourself.
5. Hang the paper/poster board some place in plain sight, where you can see it every day.
6. Spend at least five minutes every day focused on your dream wall. Think about what actions need to be taken to accomplish or achieve

the things on your wall. Then start creating action steps to implement immediately.

> **"The future belongs to those who believe in the beauty of their dreams."**
>
> **- Eleanor Roosevelt**

Secret #22

Develop Good Study Habits

Habits can be your best friend or your worst enemy. The question you need to constantly ask yourself is, "What type of habits am I creating for myself?"

Make it your mission to develop good study habits. This will not only assist you in getting better grades now in high school, it will also serve you when you get into higher levels of education.

Start to practice study habits that will make you a success at the college and university level. Don't simply find ways to study that work in high school where you are now; be thinking about the future. Learn and develop strategies for studying which will produce positive results for you long term.

When good study habits become second nature for you, you may be surprised by the level of success you will be able to achieve and the results you will accomplish.

> *"Coming together is a beginning; keeping together is progress; working together is success."*
>
> *- Henry Ford*

Secret #23

Clarify Your Goals

Be extremely clear about your goals for school and life and your plan to accomplish them.

Ask yourself the following questions:

1. Am I being specific and as detailed as possible in describing my objective?
2. Does the objective motivate me to take action?
3. Do I believe I can achieve the objective?
4. Can I measure the progress? Can I track the result?
5. Do I have a timetable or deadline?
6. How and when will I evaluate the progress?
7. What do I need to reassess as I continue to move forward toward my objective?

"If you don't know where you are going, any road will get you there."

- Lewis Carroll

"*Our greatest glory is not in never falling, but in rising every time we fall.*"

- Confucius

Secret #24

Be Victorious

No matter what you are experiencing in your life, always remember you are a champion. You are not a victim of your circumstances or situation ... You are a victorious person.

Be victorious every day, in everything you do.

When you believe you are victorious, you will act like you are victorious, then you will experience victory in your life.

Victory in your academic life.

Victory in your arts and music life.

Victory in your sports life.

Who doesn't want a victory?

The way to win in life and experience victory on a consistent basis is to first. Be victorious. Believe you are victorious. Better yet, know you are victorious.

Say it every day, "I know, that I know, that I know I am victorious in every area of my life." - JFP

www.JerryPoe.com

> **"Joy comes from using your potential."**
>
> **- Will Schultz**

Secret #25

Tap into Your Learning Style

Everyone processes information differently. Identify your ideal learning style. Are you a visual learner? Are you an auditory learner? Or are you a kinesthetic learner?

Look for ways to learn that match your learning style. This will enable you to process information faster. Forcing yourself to learn in a way that is not natural for you will only lead to difficulty and frustration. Find learning tools or resources to assist you in processing information in a manner that works best for you.

In today's world those who can process information the fastest will have a competitive advantage over everyone else because things are changing at a faster rate than ever before.

Find faster ways to learn!

"The faster you learn, the faster you implement, the faster you get results." – JFP

www.JerryPoe.com

"*A diamond is a chunk of coal that made good under pressure.*"

- Anonymous

Secret #26

What Do You Want & Why Do You Want It?

Two important questions you need to always ask yourself are ...

- What do I want (in life, out of school or this friendship, etc.)?
- Why do I want it?

If you don't know what you want, it's impossible to get it or ask for it.

Knowing why you want it reveals your driving force behind your desire and can be used as motivation to push you forward to accomplish your objective.

"If you care enough for a result, you will most certainly attain it."

- William James

> *"Life is not a matter of holding good cards, but sometimes, playing a poor hand well."*
>
> *- Jack London*

www.JerryPoe.com

Secret #27

Relationships Always Change

One constant in life has always been and always will be change. This fact is especially true for relationships. No matter what type of relationship you are involved in, whether it's a friendship or something more serious, remember relationship always change.

One of the main reasons that relationships change is people change. We get older and experience different aspects of life. We develop different interests and different feelings.

Regardless of how you feel about a person today, be aware those feelings can change. So when you make decisions, base them on what's best for you and your future.

Knowing relationships always change is important to remember so that you won't be shocked, upset, or unprepared when they do.

Change is a normal part of life. Learn to adapt quickly and make adjustments.

> *"To win...you've got to stay in the game...."*
>
> *- Claude M. Bristol*

Secret #28

Get Good at Both Written & Verbal Communication

We will always be judged by our ability to communicate effectively. Whether you believe this to be right or wrong ... it just is. How well you speak and how well you write create impressions in the minds of everyone you interact with.

People will make determinations about who you are as a person and your credibility based on your ability to communicate. Communication skills are used to assess your education level, people skills, likeability, honesty, and trust levels.

Being able to effectively communicate verbally and in the written word will be one of the best skill sets you can ever develop if you want to succeed in this society. It doesn't matter what direction you take in the future; communication is a transferable skill needed in all areas of life.

Secret #29

Catch the Clues in the Teacher's Lesson Plan

Use the lesson plan to find the short- and long-term assignments.

Build your schedule backwards from the end of the school year.

Break down the lesson plan into check points from the final to midterm to the start of the school year. Turn the months into weeks and the weeks into daily check points. This will enable you to stay on track throughout the school year.

"Nothing is particularly hard if you divide it into small jobs."

- Henry Ford

Secret #30

Understand the Path You're On

Do you know what the future holds for you?

Can someone really predict the future?

The answer is a big YES.

You can predict the future based on the life path a person is on or direction they're headed in.

Do you know what the future holds for the path you're on? What direction are you headed in?

Are you moving toward an empowering, positive future? If not, you still have time to change your path or direction.

No matter what path you are on, you must remember to include all the good and bad experiences that are consequences of your journey and prepare yourself for the sacrifices you will have to make along the way.

"*We are what we repeatedly do. Excellence, then, is not an act, but a habit.*"

- Aristotle

www.JerryPoe.com

Secret #31

Stress Less

Find ways to relax and de-stress every day.

1. Set time aside each day to relax. Find a quiet space to clear and calm your mind and relax your body for at least 15 minutes.
2. Get the amount of sleep you need each night.
3. Practice deep breathing.
4. Find something to laugh about.
5. Do something you love or enjoy. Have fun.
6. Listen to music that uplifts and soothes you.
7. Read an empowering book, poem, or quotes.

"It is not how much we have, but how much we enjoy...."

- Charles H. Spurgeon

> **"Do not wish to be anything but what you are, and try to be that perfectly."**
>
> **- St. Francis de Sales**

Secret #32

Become Highly Effective at Researching a Topic & Documenting Your Sources

At some point in your academic life, you will be required to write a report or term paper. Most likely you will be asked to write more than one. Because we know this is an inevitable reality for us, it would be wise to develop the skills needed to succeed in this endeavor.

The best way to become highly effective at researching is to find someone who is already good at it. The best place to find a good researcher is where we actually go to do the research. Make your local or school librarian your ally. Help them help you, by allowing them to show you the best sources for the information you are seeking. Allow them to point you in the right direction and show you how to effectively use the library to your advantage. Ask them questions. Ask them for how-to tips. Use them as a resource to find the information you need.

Secret #33

Discover Your Passion

The critical factors in success are passion and purpose. When you discover your passion in life, it will help lead to your purpose in life. Your passion is usually tied into your purpose. Knowing your passion and your purpose are essential to charting the right course or direction for your life.

What interests you in life?

What do you love to do?

What drives you?

If you could do only one thing for the rest of your life, what would it be?

Find a way to turn your passion and purpose into a profitable career.

"Big things are never done by little people. However, it often takes a big person to do little things."

- Anonymous

Secret #34

Where Will You Be This Time Next Year?

As we bring each year to a close and usher in another full of promise, adventure, and possibility, we ponder the course of events that have led us to this moment in time. Did the year end the way you wanted? Did you receive the results you desired? If the answer is yes, then take a moment to celebrate and reward yourself. However, if the answer is no, then how are things going to be different next year? What are you going to do so that you can answer **YES** next year?

In order for the results to change, we must change. When we change our thinking, we change our choices, which will change the results we experience. If someone would ask, "Where will you be this time next year?" would you be able to answer? This is a clue to our level of thinking. If we do not know our destination, it will be challenging to end up in the right place. The one thing we can do to make sure next year exceeds this year is to create a plan for our lives.

I call it a LIFEPRINT. Take the time to draft the plan for your life. The best time to start the year is when it's already finished. Have it finished in your mind and on paper. When you see where you want to go, then you know what direction to take.

> *"No matter what your past has been, you have a spotless future."*
>
> *- Anonymous*

Secret #35

Motivate Yourself & Eliminate Procrastination

Develop a process for activating yourself to take action and for getting into a work flow for homework, projects, and challenging tasks.

1. Try to take breaks every half an hour. Get up and walk or do some stretching exercises.
2. Reward yourself once you have completed your work.
3. Find your optimal workspace where you can focus and eliminate distractions.

"We first make our habits, and then our habits make us."

- John Dryden

Secret #36

Define Yourself for Yourself

No one knows you better than you know yourself. You know what you like or don't like. You know what interests you or not. So don't let other people define or label you.

The worst thing you can do is allow someone else to determine who you are and what you are about. Don't let people put you in a box.

Letting someone tell you who are you and how you should act is self-defeating. If you let this happen, you give your personal power away to them.

Define yourself for yourself. Who do you want to be in life? Where do you want to go in life? What are your dreams and aspirations?

Be your own person. Be an individual.

Who are you? What are you about?

Write an empowering description of yourself.

Secret #37

... More than a Title or Position

Leadership is more than a title or position. Leadership is who you are as a person. The title you have does not make you a leader. The position you are in does not make you a leader.

Who you are as a person determines whether you are a leader or not. How high is your level of leadership?

Leadership is what you do.

Leadership is how you live.

Leadership is what you say.

Make leadership your lifestyle.

"Ability may take you to the top, but it takes character to keep you there."

- John Wooden

Secret #38

Seek Out Extra Credit Opportunities

You never know when an extra credit point or two will come in handy.

Look for ways to create extra credit opportunities.

Ask your teacher if he/she has opportunities for extra credit.

> *"We tend to get what we expect."*
>
> *- Norman Vincent Peale*

Secret #39

Know the School Is Intended to Help You

The purpose of the school is to educate and graduate productive individuals.

Become familiar with your guidance counselor and the services in the guidance office at your school.

If you need a tutor ... ask for one.

If you need help with study skills ... ask the teacher or guidance counselor for suggestions.

Secret #40

This Is Only the Beginning

There is so much more to life after high school than you could ever imagine. While you are going through school, you really don't realize life has barely begun. The drama, challenges, and politics of high school will seem so trivial once you graduate. You will be surprised by how much life changes once you leave high school.

So no matter what you are experiencing in school right now ... whether you're having a tough time, just getting by, or enjoying every minute. Remember this is only the beginning of your journey ... things will change. Life has more in store for you.

Don't make high school the high point or the low point of your life. It's only the beginning, and you have the power to write the next chapter.

Secret #41

Remember What's Important

What you feel and think are so important in your life today, will not be as important tomorrow, next week, next month, or next year. The key to success is to remember what is really important in your life—what things are going to have a long-term impact on your life.

Ask yourself, "What is really important in my life today?"

Only you can truly assess what is important in your life. Only you can set and establish the right priorities for your life.

Are the opinions of your friends or classmates really that important to your life long term?

Is being popular really that important to your life long term?

Is having the latest gadget, clothes, or shoes really that important to your life long term?

Focus on what really matters in life ...
family, maximizing your potential,
developing your talents, succeeding
academically, and planning for your
future after high school.

> *"That best portion of a good
> man's life? His little,
> nameless, unremembered
> acts of kindness and of love."*
>
> *- William Wordsworth*

Secret #42

Get to Know Your Teachers

Building a connection with your teachers outside regular class time will definitely give you an advantage.

Find out what groups or clubs they advise.

Do they coach any sports?

Find a common ground to build rapport with them.

Get your teachers on your side.

Secret #43

If It Is Going to Be, It Is Up to Me

Excuses. Excuses. Excuses.

You can always find an excuse for not getting the result you desire. You can always find an excuse for not taking action.

If you want to be a successful leader, learn to eliminate excuses. You can make excuses or take action. You cannot do both.

Top leaders understand if it is going to happen, it is up to them to take action. They do not wait for someone to make it happen for them.

If not you, then who will do it?

If not now, then when will it get done?

"Once you are comfortable with an excuse, it becomes part of your life story." - JFP

Secret #44

Become Active in the Community

Get involved in a community activity. Giving back to others is a wonderful experience and builds character.

You may be surprised at how much you will learn about yourself and people when you work with community service organizations. You will learn how to appreciate where you are in life and what you have in life. You start to take less for granted.

As an added benefit it also looks good on a college application and resume.

"Do all the good you can, By all the means you can, In all the ways you can, In all the places you can, At all the times you can, To all the people you can, As long as you ever can."

- John Wesley

www.JerryPoe.com

Secret #45

Education Is More than a Grade

Do not get caught up in the game of just making the grade. Education is not memorizing facts and cramming information into your short-term memory in order to pass a test. Education is about learning so that you can find your own greatness.

What are you discovering about yourself?

Who are you becoming?

Are you learning to be a critical thinker and develop your own philosophy for life?

Are you expanding your perspective to see more possibilities for yourself?

Are you finding your own voice?

Yes, grades are important as they are used to measure our progress. However, make you sure you are becoming wiser and more knowledgeable in the process of making the grade.

Secret #46

Have Sight beyond Sight

People who have sight beyond sight are visionary leaders. They conceive or perceive things that have not happened yet. In one of his speeches, Martin Luther King Jr. said, "I've been to the mountaintop and I've seen the Promised Land. I might not get there with you."

Leaders have developed the ability to see things before the people that they are leading can see it. Even though the people who are being led may not see it, they'll go with their leader because they believe in that leader.

Use your imagination to create the reality that you live in. John F. Kennedy said, "We're going to go to the moon." Even though no one had ever gone to the moon, he had already conceived the idea. Once it was conceived ... it eventually became a reality.

We have the ability to take what we can see internally and see it as real; you have to see it to the point where it is real to you. Once it becomes real to you, you can take that thing and make it a reality so that everyone else can see.

People who have sight beyond sight are creative leaders. For example, most people saw a block of stone. Michelangelo saw the sculpture *David* in the block of stone.

Leaders have the ability to see things others cannot see and believe things others cannot believe, and they take action even when people are going to attack them. Not everyone is going to see or believe; therefore, they are not going to go with you. But when it becomes a reality, everybody wants to go with you.

> *"Let me tell you the secret that has led to my goal: My strength lies solely in my tenacity."*
>
> *- Louis Pasteur*

Secret #47

Consider It All Joy

Things are going to happen in life that are going to challenge you. They are going to take you to a place that you have never been before. When we start to get challenged or go to places that we have never been before, we experience discomfort.

However, if you have the ability to consider it all joy, these uncomfortable experiences can become fun. Find a way to turn your life experiences into joyful experiences.

Everyone has different ideas of what is joyful. What is joyful to you?

Some people enjoy winning games and solving puzzles. So when things get a little rough, they find a way to turn their situation into a game. The game is to overcome the challenge.

A game is fun. If something is fun, you are more likely to do it. However, if you see something as painful, you want to avoid it.

Enjoy the journey.

> *"Do not let what you cannot do interfere with what you can do."*
> *- John Wooden*

Secret #48

Make Consistent Progress

How much progress you make is not as important as how consistent your progress is. Make something happen consistently.

Some people get frustrated. Because they cannot do something big, they do nothing. All it takes is a really small step. It does not take a big step.

Move forward in life, even if it is in small steps. Baby steps are better than taking no steps. When you are stagnant, things start to decrease.

If you were in the ocean and waiting to get rescued, your body would keep you above the water as long as it was in motion. It is when you stop moving that you sink, drown, and die. The key is to keep making consistent progress.

"Potential has a shelf life; at some point potential has to turn into productivity." – JFP

www.JerryPoe.com

"*Even if you're on the right track, you'll get run over if you just sit there.*"

- Will Rogers

Secret #49

Implement Immediately

Successful leaders do not wait to take action. They get an idea and they start applying it to their life in some area.

You do not have to apply every idea at once. Take one secret, one strategy, or one concept and start using it immediately.

Focus on:

- Completion
- Execution
- Realization
- Application

Implementation is critical. When you get new information, apply it. Applying new ideas immediately increases your retention.

People retain only about 7–10 percent of what they hear, read, and see for the first time. However, if you implement information within a period of 24–48 hours, you increase your chances of remembering it by 80 Percent.

www.JerryPoe.com

Get into action! The faster you apply, the faster you get a result. The longer you wait, the less likely you are to get it done.

> *"A thought which does not result in an action is nothing much, and an action which does not proceed from a thought is nothing at all."*
>
> *- Georges Bernanos*

Secret #50

Live a Compounded Life

What you learn in life is based on two things: your own experiences and the experiences of other people.

If you learn life lessons based only on your experiences, you limit your capacity for wisdom. However, if you take other people's life experiences and learn from them, and combine those lessons with your own experiences, you will increase your capacity for understanding and wisdom exponentially.

You can learn from anyone's life experience. Some people are examples to model. Some are lessons of caution.

When you read an autobiography of a successful person, when you listen to audio programs from a successful person, when you study people's lives, you learn from their experiences, which enhance yours.

www.JerryPoe.com

"Time has no meaning in itself unless we choose to give it significance."

- Leo Buscaglia

Secret #51

Pursue the Route of Least Resistance

Do not force things to work. Find the most effective option. Focus on your intention and result, rather than the mechanism or method used. There is always more than one way to accomplish the objective. Which one has the least resistance or opposition?

Find what works best for you. Develop your own leadership style and system based on your natural talents and skills.

Look for opportunities to create cooperation.

Make adjustments. Adjust your plan according to the circumstances instead of forcing your original plan to work.

"Men are born to succeed, not to fail."

- Henry David Thoreau

"Always do more than is required of you."

- George S. Patton

Secret #52

Utilize Passion

Passion is enthusiasm.

Passion is contagious.

People will want to be a part of whatever you are passionate about because they will feel your passion.

When people sense your passion for an idea or concept, they are more likely to get involved and participate.

Your passion for an objective builds commitment in yourself and others. The higher the level of passion, the higher the level of commitment. Human beings are emotional—most people are emotionally driven. Use your passion to stir their emotions toward positive action.

Have zeal.

"Impossible is a word only to be found in the dictionary of fools."

- Napoleon Bonaparte

www.JerryPoe.com

> **"Example is not the main thing in influencing others. It is the only thing."**
>
> **- Albert Schweitzer**

Secret #53

Act on Purpose

Everything has a purpose. Everything has a plan. Everything is done for a reason. Nothing is done by accident. Everything is structured.

Do you approach life or any endeavor with "Let me just see what happens" or "Let me make things happen"?

When you say, "Let me just see what happens," anything you get will be satisfactory. Anything you get will be up to your expectations because you do not have any expectations.

When you act on purpose, you plan things out. You know your outcome ahead of time. You are very intentional in everything you do because there is a reason behind it.

Focus on your outcome. Take time to sit and think about what you want things to be like.

Ask yourself:

- "What is the reason that I am

doing this?"
- "Does whatever I am about to do line up with my purpose?"

When you act on purpose, you are determined, focused, persevering, persistent, and resolute. You do not allow obstacles to deter you from where you want to go. Your purpose is the driving force inspiring your actions.

Because you know where you are going and why you are going, as challenges occur and roadblocks get in your way, you can take a detour and still arrive at the destination.

> *"Success is the sum of small efforts -- repeated day in and day out."*
>
> *- Robert Collier*

Secret #54

Show Empathy

The basic factors behind empathy are understanding and compassion. Being empathetic means you are able to see things from multiple perspectives.

In order to show empathy, you must develop patience and tolerance, and you must not judge other people. When you judge others, you are basically saying that they should be making their decisions in life based on what you know.

When you look at a person, are you looking at them from your knowledge and experience in life or with the awareness that their knowledge and experience in life is different from yours?

The more understanding you are of others, the more they will want to be around you because people seek to be understood. We are looking for somebody to listen to us. We are looking for somebody to show us compassion and appreciation.

"Success seems to be largely a matter of hanging on after others have let go."

- William Feather

Secret #55

Consistently Make Life Assessments

Ask yourself the following questions (every 6 to 12 months) to assess where you are in life and determine if you are on the right track.

What is the most important achievement in my life thus far?

What would I do if I knew I couldn't fail?

What do I want more of in my life right now and in the future?

I'd like my family and friends to remember me as ...?

What do I need to do more of, or get better at, or stop doing in order to experience myself as a happier, more successful, and contributing person?

If I could change one thing in my life for the better out of this experience, what would it be?

List some ways in which you have turned your back, neglected boundaries, or have used the excuse, "I don't know how!"

List some ways in which you have lowered your standards.

What is currently preventing you from reaching your goal?

> *"Chance favors the prepared mind."*
>
> *- Louis Pasteur*

Ideas and Insights

Write down your ideas/insights and how you plan to implement them.

Ideas and Insights

Write down your ideas/insights and how you plan to implement them.

Ideas and Insights

Write down your ideas/insights and how you plan to implement them.

Empower and Equip Others!
Share this Book

What I Wish I Knew When I Was in ... College

77 Secrets EVERY Student Needs to Know about Succeeding in School, Leadership, Life, and a Career

How great would it be if you were given a manual to guide you through every aspect of your life that lay ahead of you? Give yourself the winning edge. Crack the code to success in school, leadership, life, and a career by reading the tips shared throughout this book. These quick tips are easy to read, understand, and more importantly apply immediately. Go ahead and get started!

Special Quantity Discounts

2 – 20 Books	$15.00 ea.
21 – 99 Books	$14.00 ea.
100 – 499 Books	$13.00 ea.
500 – 999 Books	$12.00 ea.
1000+ Books	$11.00 ea.

To Place an Order
Call (484) 301-0763

www.JerryPoe.com